SOCCER TALK

By Marilyn Sherman

ISBN 0-15-313968-4

Ordering Options
ISBN 0-15-314006-2 (Grade 6 Collection)
ISBN 0-15-314172-7 (package of 5)

1 2 3 4 5 6 7 8 9 10 026 99 98

Miguel tied his soccer shoes and joined his team.

"This team is a bunch of losers," he heard Sam complain.

Miguel's team had lost their last four games. None of the players was excited about playing in the big tournament. At least these were the final games of the season.

1

Miguel got onto the bus. The ride to the tournament would be long— and lonely. He didn't think his English was very good yet, so he had a hard time talking with his teammates.

He took a seat by himself and opened a comic book. He pretended to read as he listened to the chatter of the other boys.

Finally, they reached the tournament. The coach led the players to a corner of a practice field. The team trudged over without much spirit. Miguel watched the players of other teams. They were bouncing balls on their knees and taking shots at the goal.

Coach Davies began his old "we can win" speech. "You are not losers," he told the players. "You just need to work together, to communicate. Talk to each other when you're on the field!"

Miguel got the feeling that Coach Davies was talking directly to him. He felt that the team blamed him for losing. "They think I can't understand the plays," he thought to himself.

Suddenly, one boy cried out, "Look, there's Raúl!" It was the immortal Raúl Pérez, a big soccer star from Chile! The team ran to see him.

A huge crowd formed around Raúl. There was a clamor among the players. They all begged for his autograph.

Miguel clutched a soccer ball. He tried to slip through the crowd. He got as close as he could. "Please—*por favor,*" he said, imploring Raúl in Spanish. "May I have your autograph?" He held out the ball.

Raúl flashed a smile. He asked Miguel his name, and the two chatted together in Spanish. Raúl gladly signed the ball.

Then he surprised Miguel by asking him to introduce him to his team. The players looked at Miguel and Raúl in amazement. They were thrilled! Miguel proudly bestowed the autographed ball on his team.

5

Then Raúl offered to give the team a few tips. He also showed them some new plays. Raúl did not speak English. Miguel translated his words for his teammates.

"*Pasa a la derecha,*" Raúl called to the players on the field. "*¡Tira!*"

"Pass right and shoot!" Miguel interpreted. Soon the team learned the Spanish commands as well as the plays.

Raúl left. The team had an hour to practice their new moves. Miguel ran down the field. He felt relaxed and excited at the same time. "Pass left—*¡Pasa a la izquierda!*" yelled Sam. Miguel swerved left around Steve and passed the ball to Sam. Sam slammed the ball into the goal. The offense cheered. The team was starting to look more like a team—and less like losers.

It was time for their first game. The players took their places on the field and faced their opponents. The center forward kicked the ball into play. Miguel's team moved in to get control of the ball. Their passes were sharp. They called out directions.

"*¡Pasa a la derecha! ¡Pasa a la izquierda!*" they yelled to each other. The other team was confused. What were these guys saying? they wondered. Miguel and his teammates knew that their new plays were working. They scored goal after goal and won the game.

The team shouted cheers and sang songs as they headed back to the bus. Miguel did his best to sing along. Just as their bus was about to leave, there was a tap on the window. It was Raúl.

"*Felicidades*—Congratulations!" he shouted.

"*Gracias*—Thank you," said Miguel with a smile. "*Adios.*"

"*¡Adios!*" the other players shouted. They waved good-bye as the bus pulled away.

Soccer Success

Use the clues on the left to fill in the blanks. The letters in the boxes spell out how the soccer team in this story achieved success.

The game Miguel plays   _ _ [   ] _ _ _

Player who guards the goal   _ [   ] _ _ _ _

Eleven players working together   _ _ _ [   ]

New boy who brings the team together   [   ] _ _ _ _ _ _

Event in which many teams compete _ _ [   ] _ _ _ _ _ _ _ _

Language Miguel and Raúl speak   _ _ _ [   ] _ _ _

Spanish word that means "good-bye" _ _ [   ] _ _

Who Mr. Davies is   [   ] _ _ _ _

Hero, star, and helper   _ [   ] _ _

Raúl's signature on the ball   _ _ [   ] _ _ _ _ _ _

What the team does after it wins   _ _ [   ] _ _ _

TAKE-HOME BOOK

[ANSWERS soccer, goalie, team, Miguel, tournament, Spanish, adios, coach, Raúl, autograph, cheers; COMMUNICATE]